D0981604

School Smarts

All the Right Answers to Homework, Teachers, Popularity, and More!

By Brooks Whitney
Illustrated by Tracy McGuinness

American Girl®

Published by Pleasant Company Publications
information, address: Book Editor, Pleasant Company
Publications, 8400 Fairway Place, P.O. Box 620998,
Middleton, Wisconsin 53562.

Visit our Web site at **americangirl.com**

Maufactured in China.
04 05 06 07 C&C 10 9 8 7
American Girl Library® is a registered trademark
of Pleasant Company.

Editorial Development: Michelle Watkins, Julie Williams
Art Direction: Kym Abrams
Design: Gina Luoma
Photography: Mike Walker, Sandy May, Paul Tryba

Permissions: pp. 6 & 96—Joe Atlas/Artville; pp. 30-31—
Text from *Across the Centuries* in Houghton Mifflin
Social Studies by Armento, et al. Copyright © 1991 by
Houghton Mifflin Company. Reprinted by permission
of Houghton Mifflin Company. All rights reserved.
Photography from Robert Harding Picture Library,
London and Comstock, Inc.

Library of Congress Cataloging-in-Publication Data
Whitney, Brooks.
School smarts : insider secrets and all the right
answers/ by Brooks Whitney; illustrated by Tracy
McGuinness. p. cm. "American girl library."
Summary: Offers advice on a variety of school-related
topics, including getting along with teachers, doing
homework, studying for tests, preparing presentations,
being popular, and more.
ISBN 1-58485-112-8 (pbk.)
   1. Study skills—Juvenile literature. 2. Teenage girls—
Social life and customs. [1. Study skills. 2. Homework.
3. Schools. 4. Conduct of life.] I. McGuinness, Tracy, ill.
II. American girl (Middleton, Wis.) III. Title.
LB1049 . W527 2000
373.18235'2—dc21
00-020111 CIP

Dear Reader,

Whether you're a B student striving to get an A or you're just looking for ways to perk up the school day, <u>School Smarts</u> has the ideas to get you started. Quiz yourself on school spirit. Have fun while getting your homework done. Find out what to do if you have too much to do. You'll also get tips on teacher trouble, the scoop on working with groups, and the secrets to popularity.

School is more than making the grade. It's a place for finding out what you like to do, trying out new ideas--and having fun, too!

Your friends at American Girl

Contents

GET IT TOGETHER 7

Too much clutter? 10

IN THE CLASSROOM 19

Teacher trouble? 24

POPULARITY 41

Take the True Friends Test. 52

HOMEWORK 59

Stuck? 69

Homework blues? 66

TAKING TESTS 73

Test tomorrow? 76

GREAT PRESENTATIONS 83

Report
due? 86

Time for school. Are you really ready?

Get It Together

Ready or Not?

Circle the answer that describes what you'd most likely do. Be honest!

1. Your teacher is giving homework directions, but you don't bother to write it all down. You'll just call somebody tonight and get the assignment.

    a. I'd never do that.

    b. I might do that.

    c. That's me.

2. You've got a new teacher: **Big Bad Barb Brown.** Mom says to give her a chance. "Yeah, right," you sigh.

    a. I'd never do that.

    b. I might do that.

    c. That's me.

3. When you get a confusing assignment, you think, "Who can understand this stuff? It sounds like some Martian language. I can't do this. Why even try?"

    a. I'd never think that.

    b. I might think that.

    c. That's me.

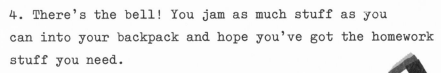

4. There's the bell! You jam as much stuff as you can into your backpack and hope you've got the homework stuff you need.

      a. I'd never do that.

      b. I might do that.

      c. That's me.

5. Your science project is due next week, but you're not worried because your partner is the smartest kid in your class. No need to work hard on this one. You've got it made.

      a. I'd never do that.

      b. I might do that.

      c. That's me.

Report Card

Mostly a's. Ready! You know that being ready means more than having your stuff organized. You're willing to take notes, give teachers a chance, ask questions when confused, and carry your fair share of the workload.	**A**
Mostly b's. Sort of ready. You know what's right, but can be tempted to let lazy habits get you off track. Shake off negative thoughts before they sink in, and be more organized. You know you can do it—you've just got to be willing to try.	**B**
Mostly c's. Not ready! Stop and smell the chalk dust. Now's the time to get into the habit of writing everything down—and double-checking that you've got what you need. Remember, too, that you can't be a good student if you pack a bad attitude.	**C**

Places, Please!

To get a fresh start, find a good place for . . .

Your *Really* Important Stuff

Always put important things that your parents need to see, like report cards, in a place they're sure to look. Hang test papers on the fridge with a magnet. Leave permission slips on the counter next to their keys.

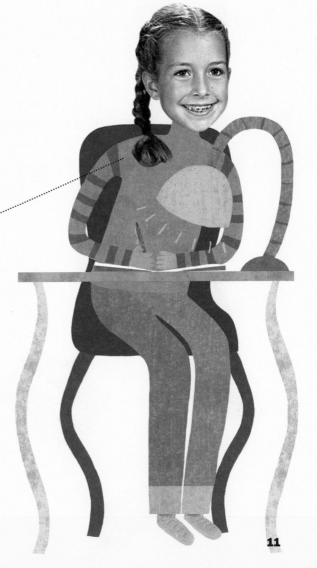

Your Other Stuff

Keep a shoe box filled with
school supplies. Store papers
you want to save or may need
again, such as book reports or
big tests, in an old backpack
or book bag. Tuck it away on a
closet shelf or under the bed.

You

Pick a quiet place away from
the center of activity. Make sure
there's enough light to work by
without straining your eyes.

Get It

School Shopping List

- ☐ folders
- ☐ lots of paper
- ☐ pencil sharpener
- ☐ a good eraser
- ☐ scissors
- ☐ a container for important papers
- ☐ calendar and assignment book
- ☐ and a trash can so you can...

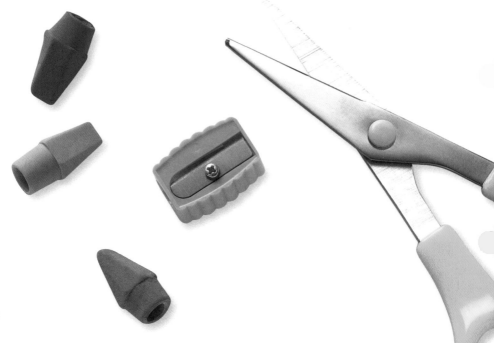

Trash It

Go on a **junk hunt** and throw out the stuff you don't need.

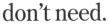

Dried-up markers

Torn folders and old school papers

Old party invitation

Pencil stubs

Out-of-date catalogues

Last week's lunch menu

Bubble gum wrappers

Doesn't your brain feel clearer already?

How is school like soccer?

Or **ballet?** Or **swimming?** Or anything else that you love or want to do? It's all about new skills, new teachers, new friends.

To do your best, you . . .

Watch the pros

Listen to the coach

Cheer for yourself and teammates

Ask questions

Set goals

Practice your skills

But most importantly, you put your whole heart into it.

Train Your Brain

Do better in school without cracking a book!

Make a date. From assignments to birthdays, write important dates— and fun dates—down in one place.

Think ahead, plan ahead. The first step to getting things done is to plan them.

guess what!

Start smart. Studies show that kids who eat breakfast do better in school.

Time out. Take a second to stamp out silly mistakes. Did you put your name on the quiz? Did you answer all the questions?

Share something fun that you've learned each day with mom or dad. Chances are it'll stick with you longer.

Z Z Z Z

Get a good night's sleep so you can rise and shine.

go girl!

Hold pep rallies in your head.

"You can do it!"

"Ace that test!"

Turn off the TV before you tune in the homework.

ZZZap!

Nice 'n neat

Nice 'n neat. Write neatly enough for your teacher to read, and try to keep papers wrinkle-free.

Fizz Ed. Keep fresh ideas burbling through your brain by getting plenty of exercise.

I think that

Express yourself! Take part in class discussions. Tell others what you think.

Pitch it. Clean clutter out of your book bag, backpack, or coat pockets every day before you leave for school.

"Here, Spot!" Have a special study spot where your mind clicks into study gear when you sit there.

Remember: You already know a lot. Use what you've got to get through new challenges.

17

Swamped!

Q: *I have a very busy schedule this year, and I'm worried that between school, sports, and all my activities, I won't be able to keep up with things.*

A: **Planning** is the key to making a busy schedule work. Figure out how long it will take you to do each thing—homework, tennis, piano practice. Then make a plan to get everything finished and **stick with it!** Keep track of your **schedule** in a planner or appointment book. Check items off as you complete them. If you find that you're still not able to **keep up**, you may be taking on too much. If that's the case, talk to your parents about helping you **cut back** on one or two activities so you'll have time for the most important thing—school.

In the Classroom

School Spirit

Do you give it all you've got or are you just hanging out?
Circle the answer that describes you best.

1. When your teacher tells everyone to sit where they want,
you grab a desk up front where you can see the board.
    a. That's me.   b. That's not me.

2. When you get a not-so-great grade on a test, you go over
it and correct your answers.
    a. That's me.   b. That's not me.

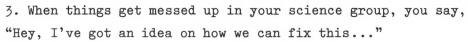

3. When things get messed up in your science group, you say,
"Hey, I've got an idea on how we can fix this..."
    a. That's me.   b. That's not me.

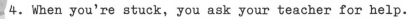

4. When you're stuck, you ask your teacher for help.
    a. That's me.   b. That's not me.

5. When your new teacher asks for volunteers to read a poem
from a book, you raise your hand to break the ice.
    a. That's me.   b. That's not me.

Report Card

5 a's. You've got **spirit!** Yes, you do. You know that it takes **more** than just brains to be a successful student. **Attitude counts!**

3 to 4 a's. That's **all right.** That's **OK.** Remember, the **more** you put into school, the more you get back. So give a **little more** and see how **far** you can go.

1 to 2 a's. Your school spirit is running **low.** Give it a boost by trying a few ideas from the quiz. The more you **participate,** the more interested you'll be and the more involved you'll feel. A little effort goes **a long way!**

Head of

Do you have what it takes to get to the head of the class?

START

bee happy
You're the spelling bee champ! Go ahead 2 spaces.

clock watcher
Stare at the clock longer than at the blackboard. Go back 1 space.

psst hey

A+

busy body
Ask the girl behind you, "What grade did you get?" Go back 1 space.

extra credit
Do three extra math problems to boost your grade. Go ahead 2 spaces.

chatty cathy
Get caught passing notes. Go back 2 spaces.

lost in space
Get called on in the middle of a daydream. Go back 1 space.

the moocher
Borrow paper for a pop quiz because you didn't bring any. Go back 1 space.

the Class

Find some dice and play the game!

Show 'n tell

Share pictures of the Grand Canyon with the class. Go ahead 2 spaces.

annoying Questions

"Is this going to be on the test?" Lose a turn.

to the rescue

Help a classmate with a long division problem. Go ahead 1 space.

I know I know

know-it-all

Blurt out an answer before being called on. Go back 1 space.

Pick me

Volunteer to go to the blackboard. Go ahead 1 space.

make someone's day

Ask the new kid to join you for lunch. Go ahead 1 space.

quiz

play catch-up

Ask to borrow notes from the day you were absent. Go ahead 1 space.

class clown

Make goofy faces at your best friend. Her giggles disrupt class. Lose a turn.

FINISH

Teacher Trouble?

My teacher yelled at people for no reason, and she totally had teacher's pets. My friends and I were really having a problem with it. So we went to see the school counselor. She gave us helpful ways to deal with our anger and frustration.
Michelle, **Washington**

Last year I had a teacher who gave lots of homework. She made me mad, but I decided to focus on the good side of her instead of the bad. I found out that she was really funny, and that she gave the homework to help us practice what we learned.
Kellie, **Massachusetts**

Sometimes my teacher talks too fast. But if I raise my hand and tell her, she'll slow down.
Lindsey, **Illinois**

I used to hate math. I thought my teacher wasn't good. But later I realized that I was being negative and not open to learning. So I tried doing things his way and now math is 100% easier!

Rachel, **California**

My teacher went overboard with homework. Since I was involved in lots of after-school activities, it was tough for me. I talked to my teacher about it, and she started staying after school to help me. Sometimes I had to miss my activities, but I realized that school comes first!

Lauryn, **New York**

I used to get really frustrated because I thought my teacher gave way too much homework. When I talked to her about it, she said, "I don't give a lot of homework. It's just that you don't finish your work in class." I realized she was right and cut down on my talking. It worked!

Chelsie, **Ohio**

Talk It Out

There's a **wrong** way and a **right** way to talk to a teacher.

This book is boring.

Plan your words.

I ... uh, um ... don't really get it.

Be specific.

I'm having trouble getting into this book.

I don't understand dividing fractions.

Your tests are too hard.

Offer a suggestion.

Could we have a review day?

I can't keep up because you give too much homework.

Refrain from blame.

I can't seem to finish all of my homework. Do you have any suggestions?

All the good research paper topics are taken.

Ask for advice.

Can you recommend a topic that I'd be interested in writing about?

BIG truth

↓

Teachers want you to do well.

Having a problem? Talk to them.

Learn It

There are **3** ways to get things to sink in.

1. Do It!

Hands-on work helps you learn new things.

field trip

science experiment

acting in school play

2. See It!

You soak up information by reading, watching, and looking at everything around you.

maps

books

newspapers

photos

3. Hear It!

Your ears are always listening for new sounds and signals.

S-P-E-L-L-I-N-G

teacher speaking

recordings   music

Mini-Quiz

How do you learn best?

Q: When you get a new board game, you like to learn how to play by...

a. having someone tell you the directions.
   You learn best by hearing it.

   This is how you do it

b. reading the directions yourself.
   You learn best by seeing it.

c. playing with someone who knows how.
   You learn best by doing it.

A: Whether it's one way or a combination of ways, knowing what works best helps you take it all in and remember it.

Reading Tips

Coming Attractions

Chapter introductions often give you background information or an interesting glimpse at what you're going to learn.

L E S S O N 2

The Inca

The young Inca and his fellow workers walked up to the next boulder to be moved. It was as tall as three men. Working side by side, the men wrapped a thick rope around the massive rock. At the leader's signal, they gripped the rope and began to pull. The young man grunted. His muscles strained and the palms of his hands burned. Sweat poured down his face. Slowly the boulder inched closer to the fortress. Finally, the leader signaled them to stop.

The man sat down to rest. He watched as other workers pounded and sculpted the boulder with big stone hammers. Then, with a mixture of sand and water, they all rubbed the rock until it was very smooth on four sides. When joined, the squared boulder would fit tightly with the others.

The Inca built the massive stone fortress of Sacsahuaman (sak sa wah MAN) during the 1400s. It was built just north of their capital city Cuzco in western South America. The fortress not only protected the Inca from their enemies but survived several powerful earthquakes. This is a remarkable fact, since the Inca used no mortar to join the boulders together. The fortress was one of the many technological achievements of the Inca, who conquered and ruled one of the largest empires in the Americas.

Mystery Words

If you come across a word you don't know, jot it down quickly and keep reading. After you've finished the section, look the word up and reread the passage. It'll make more sense that way!

Q & A

Textbook chapters often have questions at the end. Reading them first will highlight the important things you should think about while reading.

1. **FOCUS** In what ways were the Inca a advanced civilization?
2. **CONNECT** How did the Inca metho other tribes differ from the Aztec me
3. **GEOGRAPHY** How did altitude and ter agriculture?
4. **SOCIAL SYSTEMS** What was everyday

Easy as Pie

Don't skip photos, captions, pie charts, maps, bar graphs, and timelines. They offer another way of looking at the information.

was thin and didn't receive enough rainfall. The Inca carried topsoil and gravel from the more fertile lowlands to the hillsides. There, they packed it into narrow farming terraces like the ones pictured above. To protect against drought, the Inca constructed elaborate canal systems for irrigation.

The government built huge warehouses to store surplus food in case of emergencies such as crop failure or war. The quipu camayocs recorded how much food was stored and where it was stored. Because the government distributed food and goods to the people, free trade and huge markets like those the Aztec enjoyed did not exist in the Inca Empire. ■

▲ *Inca terraces were such an effective farming technique that they are still used in modern-day Peru.*

■ *Why was Inca agriculture so productive?*

Fancy Type

Words in bold or italic type almost always mean very important information!

n the low valleys,
aize (corn), beans,
he mountains, they
d alpacas for wool
growing of crops
height of the land
l economy.
e able to grow sur-
ood by using very
g techniques.
niques was **ter-**
soil on the
the highlands

Ancestors

noners
ood for the
oners helped
s. To learn

more about an Inca city, see A Closer Look on page 434.

Other commoners paid their tribute by making pieces of art and

433

Two American Empires

ommon people who lived in the Inca Empire?
RITICAL THINKING Why do you think the Inca wor-
d their ancestors?
ITY Choose a city that you feel best illustrates
life in the United States. Make A Closer Look for the
city you chose using photographs from magazines.

435

Two American Empires

Test Yourself

How do you know what you just read has really sunk in? Try to summarize it in your own words. If you can't, read it again.

Listening Tips

Engage Your Brain

Hearing is different from listening. Hearing means that sounds are coming into your ears. Listening means that you're *thinking* about those sounds.

Picture It

Visualize, or create a picture in your mind about what's being said.

Take Notice

Pay attention to your teacher's voice. Chances are it'll get louder when she's talking about something you really need to understand.

Keep Moving

Taking notes, raising your hand, asking questions, and going to the blackboard will help you concentrate and keep you from daydreaming.

WARNING: If you don't understand something, ask your teacher to explain it before she moves on or you'll become buried with information.

Focus

Keep your eyes on the speaker, and block out distractions.

Great Notes

Date your notes.

Write down general ideas, dates.

Shorten long words.

Add doodles of maps or diagrams.

Put stars by important information.

Underline new words and names of important people.

Tues., Oct. 19

The Inca
A.D. 1230–1525
Empire began to expand in A.D. 1453

Lived in Andes Mtns, South America

Empire included parts of Colombia, Ecuador, Peru, Bolivia, Chile, and Argentina

Spoke language called Quechua, ha no written language

Machu Picchu, mountaintop Incan ci discovered in A.D. 1911

Don't try to write down every word the teacher says. Listen for the impor-tant stuff and drop words like "a" and "the."

Keep related ideas together.

Put question marks by any points you need more information about.

Built 14,000 miles of roads

Inca were skilled stonemasons

Farmed land using irrigation system, cut terraces into hillsides, crops included corn, cotton

Potatoes first came from Andes Mtns.

? ?

Raised llamas and alpacas for wool

Go over notes after class and highlight main points.

Inca conquered by Spanish conquistador Pizarro in A.D. 1532

Group Scoop

1. Agree on your goal.

2. Brainstorm.

3. Listen and ask questions.

Got a group project? Try these teamwork tips for making it great!

4. Decide on a plan.

What's the best way to do it?

PLAN A PLAN B PLAN C

5. Take notes.

We decided to put out collection boxes.

6. Write down what you'll need.

Anything else?

☐ Posters
☐ large boxes
☐ flyers

7. Pick a leader.

I'll keep everything together.

BORN LEADER

8. Give everyone a job to do.

9. Make a timeline.

10. Check on your progress from time to time.

Group Gripes

Watch out for these common trouble spots.

When in doubt, vote—out loud, by a show of hands, or by secret ballot on paper.

It's O.K. to disagree—just make sure you disagree with the idea, not the person who suggested it.

If someone slacks off, review with the group what everyone's job is.

Picked On?

Q: I think my teacher hates me. Whenever I ask a question, he acts like I'm really stupid. I can't figure out what's wrong.

A: There may be nothing wrong! Look closely at your teacher's behavior. If he snaps at others, it's a sign that he's just naturally stern. If he seems to pick on you, though, take an honest look at yourself. Do you ask him to repeat things you would have heard if you'd been listening? How's your attitude? Changing the way you act may change the way your teacher responds. But whatever happens, don't let fear stop you from asking questions when you need to. Raise your hand or write your questions down. It's your teacher's job to make sure you understand him—and it's your job to speak up when you don't.

Popularity

What Makes a Girl Popular?

Rank the qualities below from 1 to 10, with 1 being the most important.

Cool Clothes

Pretty

Interesting

Good Grades

Good at Sports

Has the Newest Stuff

Kind

Funny

Everyone Wants 2 Bee Her

List 'em here:

1. ....
2. ....
3. ....
4. ....
5. ....
6. ....
7. ....
8. ....
9. ....
10. ....

Now turn the page to see what other girls say about being popular.

Girl Talk

Cool clothes are normally what make a girl popular. But by showing your inner qualities, you'll be respected in a different, better way. Being funny is my number one priority!

Sophia, **Oregon**

I think being popular stinks because you have to live up to everyone's expectations.

Ashley, **California**

When someone says "popular," people always think "mean" or "snobby." But at my school, a lot of the girls are popular because they have a lot of friends—and they got friends by being kind!

Lauren, **Texas**

Some girls are popular because they're pretty and have cool clothes and all the newest stuff. I wish things were different, but they aren't.

Anna, **Ohio**

I think popularity should be based on how fun or truthful you are, not by the way you look or dress.
Leigh, Missouri

I think what makes girls popular is that they're not afraid to be themselves.
Miri, Maryland

At my school, if you don't play sports, you're not cool. I don't play sports, but people who know me think I'm pretty cool. People shouldn't judge you until they know who you are inside.
Amber, Alabama

Girls become popular by showing off what's on the inside, not what's on the outside.
Jackie, Alberta

When you're trying to be popular, you're trying to please people. But no one can please everyone. Just be yourself!
Jennifer, Alabama

The most popular girl at my school is sort of strange. She wears clothes that aren't really in style, but they're still cool. She's nice to everyone. People like her because she has a good personality and she's interesting.
Alyson, Iowa

Psst!

Here are the real secrets to popularity:

Be kind.

Lend a helping hand.

Get involved in something
that you love to do.

Smile.
If you feel
good about yourself,
others will too!

Be yourself.
To have true friends, you
have to be the true you.

All Together?

"Some kids wanted me to tell a friend that everyone at our lunch table didn't like her. That was untrue, because I liked her. I didn't go along with them. I made the right decision, because if I'd told her, my friend would've felt bad."

Jordan
Pennsylvania

"None of the popular girls at my school want to be in the band. I do, but I'm afraid the girls will think that I'm a dork if I join the band, and I might not be popular anymore!"

Gracie
Missouri

Tell her we don't like her anymore.

What will they think?

48

There's nothing wrong with hanging out with a group of friends. But don't let the power of your group make you lose sight of what's right!

"My friends insult my teacher when he's not around. They call him bad words, but I don't agree with them. If I defend my teacher, they insult me, too. But I refuse to go along with them, because I know how I would feel if someone called me names—sad."

Lisa
Georgia

"Sometimes kids pressure you to hang out with only the kids they like. That's not right. It makes me feel bad when they push their opinion on me as if it were better than mine."

Britta
Washington

Stand Alone

Follow Your Head

If the crowd wants to do something that doesn't seem like a good idea to you, it probably isn't. Would you be doing this if your friends weren't pressuring you? If that little voice inside your head says "no," listen!

Follow Your Heart

When the crowd makes fun of someone, put yourself in that person's shoes. How would you feel if it were you? If the answer is "not good," then don't do it. The girls who are true to themselves are happiest in the end.

Stand Up for What's Right

Tell others when you don't agree with them. Real friends won't hold it against you. In fact, they may secretly respect you. If they act mad, tell them you're sorry they're upset. But you don't have to apologize for not joining in.

BIG
Truth

Not everyone is going to like you.

No matter how friendly, caring, and thoughtful you are, some kids just aren't going to like you. Being accepted by others is what every girl wants. But understanding that others may not always accept you is the first step to being happy and comfortable with yourself. Then true friends will follow.

True Friends Test

Read the statements below with a friend in mind to find out how true she is. The more you answer "true," the stronger the friendship!

1. **You can be yourself around her. You don't have to try to impress her, or pretend to be someone you're not.**

   ☐ True   ☐ False

2. **She makes you feel good about yourself. She doesn't make fun of you or cut you down, or even follow it up with "just kidding."**

   ☐ True   ☐ False

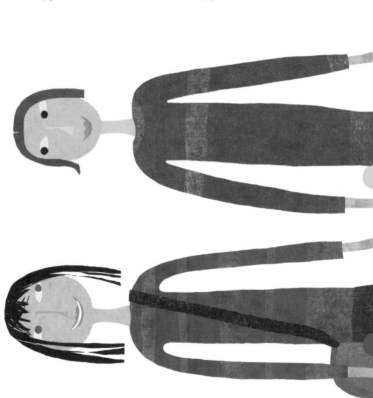

3. She supports you. Whether it's trying out for the school play or running for class president, she encourages you and wants you to succeed.

☐ True ☐ False

4. She's considerate of your needs. She listens to your problems and tries to cheer you up when you're blue.

☐ True ☐ False

5. You like who you are when you're with her. A true friend brings out the best in you—because she brings out the real you!

☐ True ☐ False

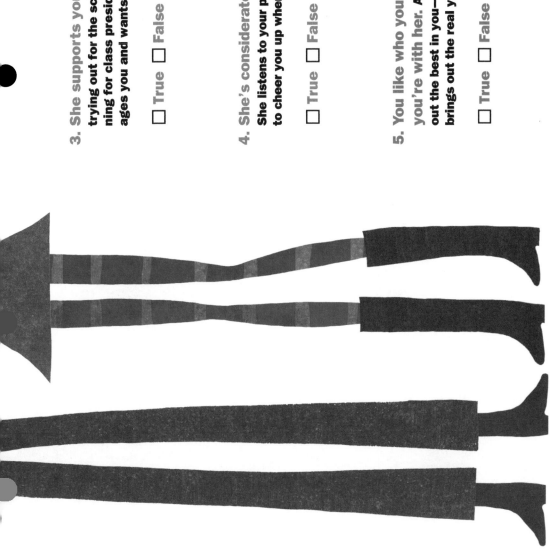

Who's New?

No one needs a good friend more than the new girl at school. Read these girls' minds and guess who's new.

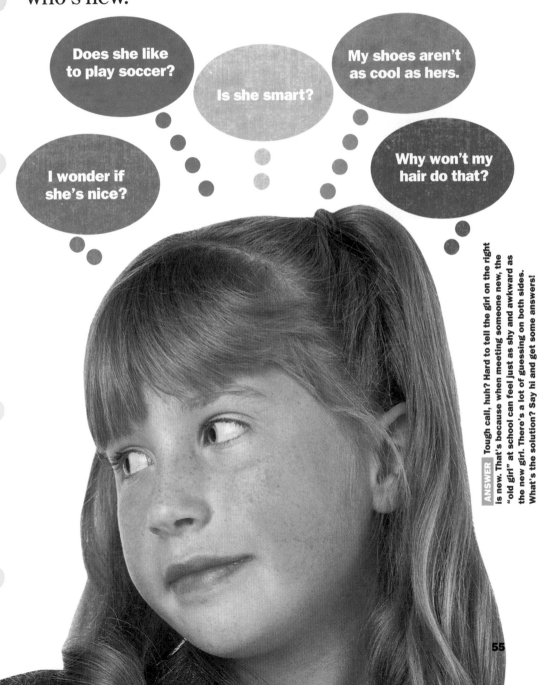

Going to a New School?

Trial Run

Ask your mom or dad to take you to your new school about a week before school starts. Take a look around and get comfortable with your new surroundings.

Old Friends

Going to a different school does not have to mean losing friends. Make a pact to keep in touch with phone calls, e-mail—even snail mail. Compare notes about your old school and your new school.

New Friends

Making new friends is easier when you have something in common to share. Join after-school clubs or activities like the school newspaper or the softball team.

Got Middle School Worries?

Find a Guide

If you know an older girl who goes to the school, ask her to show you around and introduce you to others.
Whitney, **Georgia**

Not Alone

Remember that a lot of other kids your age will be going to the new school for the first time WITH you! You'll make a ton of new friends!
Jenna, **New York**

Forget-Me-Not

Write your new locker combination on a small piece of paper. Fold it up and carry it in a locket until you memorize it.
Chelsea, **Ohio**

Take a Token

Carry something small from home that will help you feel better.
Jaqui, **California**

Trapped!

Q: I became involved with a group of friends. Everyone in the group started calling us "the best friends." The fact is, they aren't my best friends. Some of the girls are mean and are trying to grow up too fast. I'm not like that. How can I get out?

A: Often, being true to yourself takes courage. That means not doing what your friends are doing if it doesn't feel right. You don't have to stop being friends with these girls, you just need to get a little distance from them. Make plans with friends outside of the clique, or get involved in an activity that takes up a lot of your time. It will be easier to steer clear if you really do have other plans.

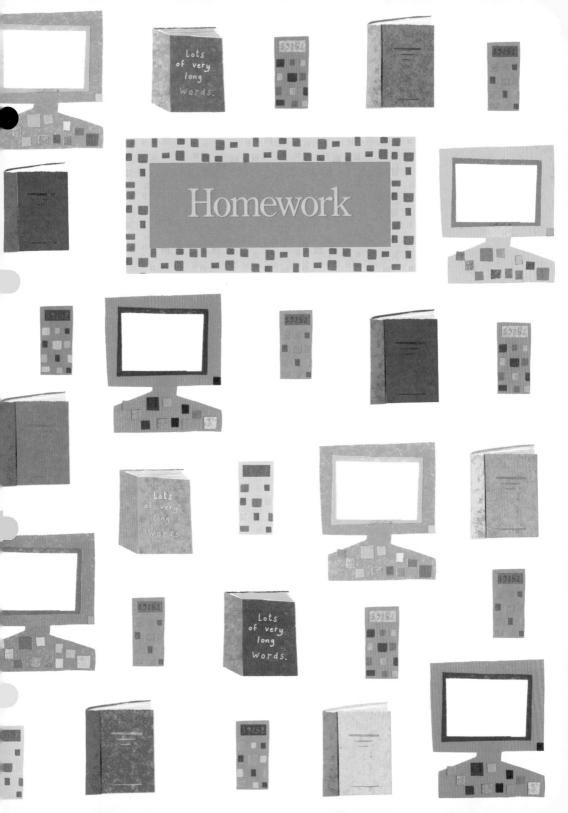

Homework

Homework IQ

1. Your favorite 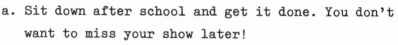 TV show is on tonight. You know the rule--no TV until you've finished your homework. You...

   a. Sit down after school and get it done. You don't want to miss your show later!

   b. Go to start it, but realize you've forgotten to write down which pages to read. So you turn on the TV.

   c. Promise to do it--right after you play a video game with your brother. But before you know it, you're watching TV, hoping no one asks about your homework.

2. You invite your best friend over to quiz you for the upcoming spelling bee. You... *hee!hee!*

   a. Have a snack and share a few giggles, then get down to work.

   b. Go to get your flash cards out of your knapsack but discover they're missing.

   c. Plan to quiz each other while you're Rollerblading together, if you remember.

3. The **big** math test you've been dreading is tomorrow. You...

    a. Feel calm and prepared. You've studied all the stuff.

    b. Sit down to study, but by the time you find a sharpened pencil, your mom is calling you for dinner.

    c. Crawl in bed with your math book. If you start studying right before you go to sleep, the answers are sure to stick.

4. Your teacher assigns a book report that is **DUE** in two weeks. You...

    a. Plan out your time so you're not rushed at the end.

    b. Go to the library to choose a book, but discover you left the list of titles in your desk.

    c. Figure you have plenty of time. Why worry about it now?

5. You have a long list of vocabulary words to define by tomorrow. It's so boring, you don't think you can stand it. You...

    a. Tackle it first while your mind is fresh and you have the energy.

    b. Sit down to do it, then realize you don't know where your dictionary is.

    c. Decide to put it off and do it the next morning before school--if you have the time.

Report Card

Mostly a's. Congratulations! Your homework style will save you time and panic attacks! Keep up the good work and you're sure to move to the head of the class. Read on to find more homework tips and tricks.	**A**
Mostly b's. Your intentions are good, but your lack of organization leaves you unprepared—and wastes a lot of time. The more organized you are, the more time you'll have to do the things you enjoy. Try some tips on getting organized on pages 10 to 15.	**B**
Mostly c's. Finding anything to do except your homework is called *procrastinating*. Procrastination is almost always accompanied by a nagging, guilty, I-should-be-doing-my-homework feeling. Try some tips on getting started on pages 64 and 65—then get to your homework before it gets to you!	**C**

too much todo?

Do This:

Don't Bite Off—
Well, You Know!

Be realistic about how much you can do after school *and* get your homework finished, too. If you have soccer practice after school and two chapters of history to read, tell your friend you'll come over tomorrow—tonight is booked!

Make a List

Write down all the assignments you need to do and when you need to do them. Then number them in the order that you plan to do them. Hint: Get the hardest work done first, and the easy stuff will be a breeze.

Make Every Minute Count

Make use of small chunks of time. Review your spelling list while waiting at the dentist's office, or have a friend quiz you on times tables at the bus stop.

Time Yourself

Set a timer for studying each subject. Limiting your time may actually help you be more productive.

Think in Pieces

Start large projects early by breaking them into batches and doing a little bit of work at a time. Get out the calendar and work backward from the due date, assigning yourself a batch a day.

Make It Fun!

Be a star. Liven up reading assignments. Pretend you're a movie actress reciting your lines.

Eat your words. Practice your spelling with alphabet cereal. If you spell the word correctly, you get to eat it!

Picture it. Decorate your flash cards. Remembering the way the card looks may help you remember the information on it.

Roll the dice. Add them together to see which homework question you should do next. 4 + 3 = question #7.

Play the part. Pretend you're a famous scientist on the verge of a big discovery or a writer working on a novel.

Hop. Recite times tables while playing hopscotch. Pick a number before you start, then multiply it by each number you land on.

ha! ha! hee! hee!

Make a tape. When you get to an important fact in your reading assignment, record it. To review the chapter, just rewind and listen.

Giggle. Read a joke from a joke book between assignments.

Get silly. Write funny sentences with your vocabulary words.

Deal 'em. Turn playing cards into a math flashcard game. Remove face cards, deal two numbered cards, and see how fast you can multiply the two numbers.

Doodle. Dot your i's with daisies on papers you don't have to turn in for a grade.

Say cheese! Keep a mirror at your desk, and give yourself a smile every now and then.

Add More Fun!

Jump! Do jumping jacks after you finish each assignment.

Be a pal. Keep your favorite stuffed animal in your lap.

Game time. Play Trivial Pursuit using flash cards as the questions.

Give me an *A*. Grab a friend and play Hangman with spelling words.

Luck out. Put on your lucky hat. Write with your lucky pen. Rub out mistakes with your lucky eraser.

Stuck?

Get Unstuck!

Get away!
Work on something else for a while, then try again 15 minutes later.

Talk it out.
Try teaching it to someone else, like a brother or a parent. Chances are it'll begin to make more sense to you.

Slow down.
Read it again—only slower this time.

Look!

Check your notes from class. Also, look back over the assignment— the answer to #8 may help you with #9.

Help?

Surf smart.

Get info from a homework helper Web site:

www.homeworkcentral.com

www.kids.infoplease.com/homework

www.ala.org (click on Kids Connect)

www.askjeevesforkids.com

E-mail the librarian at www.schoolwork.org

Hello, operator.

Call a homework hot line. Ask a teacher to recommend one.

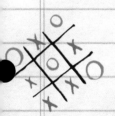

Find an expert.

Ask your sister the math whiz or your neighbor the scientist.

Feeling Dumb

Q: No matter how much I study, or how hard I try, I still don't get good grades. Am I dumb?

A: Everybody learns in different ways and at different paces. To find your style, take a look at how you're studying. Do you forget lists you've read over and over again? Try writing them instead. If that doesn't work, recite them out loud. Ask your parents, a teacher, or a guidance counselor to help you find a study style that works best for you. But remember, just as there are different ways to learn, there are different kinds of "smart." Everybody is smart in her own way. Your talents are just waiting to be discovered. Keep looking for them!

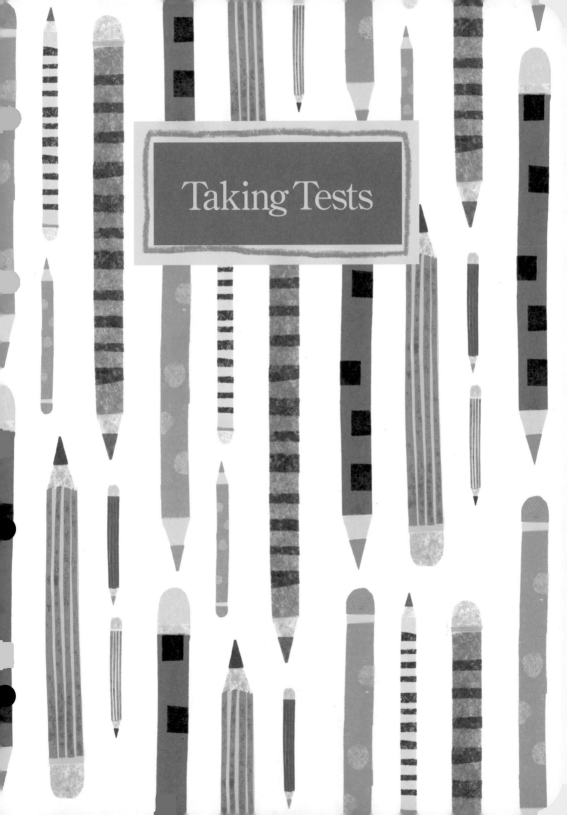

Taking Tests

What's Your Study Style?

Circle the answer that describes you best, and discover what it reveals about you!

1. You study  best ...
    a. Always at your desk.
    b. Lounging on your bed.
    c. Anywhere.
   What it might mean:
    a. You think best when things are the same. You love order!
    b. You like to be comfy while getting the work done.
    c. Nothing will 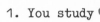 you from doing what you have to do.

2. When studying for a test, you tackle...
    a. The easy stuff first.
    b. The hard stuff first.
   What it might mean:
    a. You like to ease into things slowly and build up speed.
    b. You're not afraid to dive right in.

3. You like to study...
    a. After school.
    b. Before going to bed.
What it might mean:
    a. You like knowing everything's done. Whew!
    b. You're a night owl. You focus best when the day
       has settled.

4. You concentrate best...
    a. When it's quiet.
    b. With music or the TV on.
What it might mean:

    a. You like to focus on one thing at a time. Shhh!
    b. Background noise helps you whistle while you work.

5. You prefer to work for...
    a. Long stretches of time.
    b. Short bursts of time.
What it might mean:
    a. You have great concentration.
    b. You keep things interesting by changing your
       focus often.

6. You like to study...
    a. With a friend.
    b. Alone.
What it might mean:
    a. You like to bounce ideas and questions off others.
    b. You focus better when you're not distracted by others.

Post-It

Write key facts on Post-it notes. Stick them where you'll see them throughout the day— on your mirror, on the fridge, even inside your lunch bag.

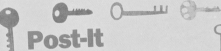

cirrus

stratus

cumulus

Link It

Link words or information you're trying to learn with something you know.

minuscule—
the size of my bedroom

Shorten It

Use mnemonic (neh-MON-ick) devices like acronyms to help you remember lists or facts.

HOMES = the five Great Lakes Huron, Ontario, Michigan, Erie, and Superior

Make It Fun!

Meet with a classmate and quiz each other on facts and figures. Pretend you're on a game show answering million-dollar questions.

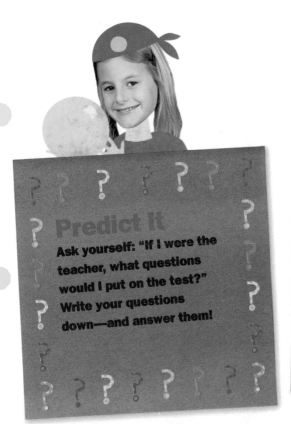

Predict It

Ask yourself: "If I were the teacher, what questions would I put on the test?" Write your questions down—and answer them!

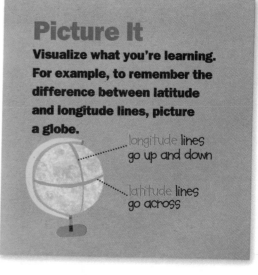

Picture It

Visualize what you're learning. For example, to remember the difference between latitude and longitude lines, picture a globe.

longitude lines go up and down

latitude lines go across

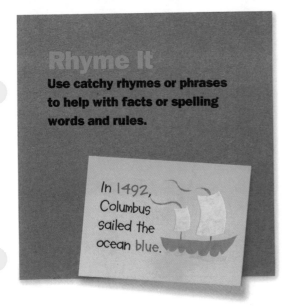

Rhyme It

Use catchy rhymes or phrases to help with facts or spelling words and rules.

In 1492, Columbus sailed the ocean blue.

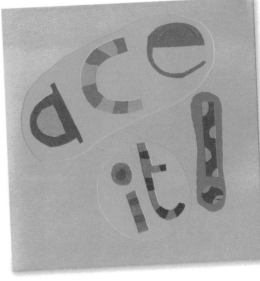

ace it!

Stay Sharp!

Try these test-taking tips.

1. ▶AG Relax. Take a deep breath.

2. ▶AG Read all of the directions--carefully.

3. ▶AG Don't be afraid to ask the teacher to explain any directions you don't understand.

4. ▶AG Read all the answer choices--even if you spot the correct answer right away.

5. ▶AG Skip over questions you can't answer quickly, then go back later.

6. ▶AG Take your time--it's not a race.

Stumped?

Here's how to troubleshoot different types of tests.

A, B, or C?

Look for the best answer by eliminating the choices you know are wrong.

Drawing a _____?

Write something down. Even if it's just the first part of the math equation or half of the essay. You might get partial credit.

True or False?

Read each statement carefully. Don't be fooled by a sentence that is only partly true.

Essay Question?

Look for key words, such as *list* or *compare*, that tell you what is wanted in your essay, and underline them. Then start writing!

AG Proofread your answers before you hand in your paper. 7

AG Go for the extra credit! 8

AG ? 2

1. To prepare for Mr. Miller's test on the Civil War, you study the test he gave to your sister's class last year on the same subject.
R U cheating? yes   no

Answer: NO. One advantage to having an older brother or sister is that you can learn from their mistakes! Reading over an old test gives you a good idea about what information is important to know. But be aware that teachers change the questions from year to year, so make sure you study your textbook and notes as well.

2. Your science experiment is all messed up. But you know what the results should be—so you write those down instead of what really happened.
R U cheating? yes   no

Answer: YES. Fudging the results or answers doesn't give you the chance to find out what went wrong. And without knowing that, you're in danger of being left behind on the next assignment. Be honest, accept your mistakes, and take the time to learn how to do things right.

3. You find a great paragraph for your research paper on a Web site. So you cut and paste the text into your document.
R U cheating? yes no

Answer: YES. Most Web sites—as well as books, magazines, encyclopedias, and newspapers—are copyrighted. That means someone owns the words. You can't steal the words. But you can put quotation marks around them and note the source. Better yet, rewrite them in your own words. Not sure what's fair? Talk to your teacher.

4. As soon as your social studies teacher hands out the test, you write mnemonic devices in the margins.
R U cheating? yes no

Answer: NO. Doing a "brain dump" of quick facts and dates as soon as you get your paper is fine. It may even free your brain up to focus on difficult questions. If your teacher is a neat freak, you may want to erase your scribbles before you turn in the test.

5. No matter which way you go at it, you just can't figure out the answer to number 3 in tonight's homework. So you ask mom for help.
R U cheating? yes no

mom can you help?

Answer: NO. It's O.K. to ask for help, as long as getting help also means you do the work yourself after someone explains it to you.

HOMES

Pressured

Q: My parents think I need to be perfect. If I get a B instead of an A, they make a big fuss over it. I know it's important to get good grades, but they're overdoing it.

A: Parents want the best for their kids, and that's what makes them push. Most parents know it's not really the grade that's important but that you tried your hardest. No one can be perfect at everything, and a B is certainly nothing to feel bad about—as long as you gave it your best effort. Talk to your parents. Explain how their pressure makes you feel—and that you feel you're doing your best.

Great
Presentations

What's Your Report Style?

1. Your teacher assigns a report on the book of your choice. You choose...

>   a. A book that you've been wanting to read.
>   b. The shortest book you can find.

2. Not only do you have to write a report, you also have to make an oral presentation to the class. You plan to...

>   a. Make note cards to help you organize and remember what you want to talk about.
>   b. Read straight from your paper.

3. The report is due in weeks, so you...

>   a. Start reading right away.
>   b. Figure you'll start in a couple of weeks. Besides, you work best under pressure.

4. When it's time to write the report, you...

>   a. Start by writing a rough draft.
>   b. Skip the rough draft. Go right to final.

5. When it comes to pr—ofreading, you ...

    a. Read your report over several times, checking

       for mistyakes.

    b. Think, "That's what they made spellcheckers

       for, right?"

Report Card

Mostly a's: You've learned the **secrets** to great report writing: pick a subject that really interests you, give yourself plenty of **time,** and get the **details** right!

Mostly b's: You may **save** time, but your report is going to show it. Take the time to **think** it through and try putting **yourself** into it more. Choose a subject or angle that's interesting to you, and you'll find that writing and presenting your topic can actually be **fun.**

Brainstorm!

Got a topic? Good. Now come up with as many questions about it as you can.

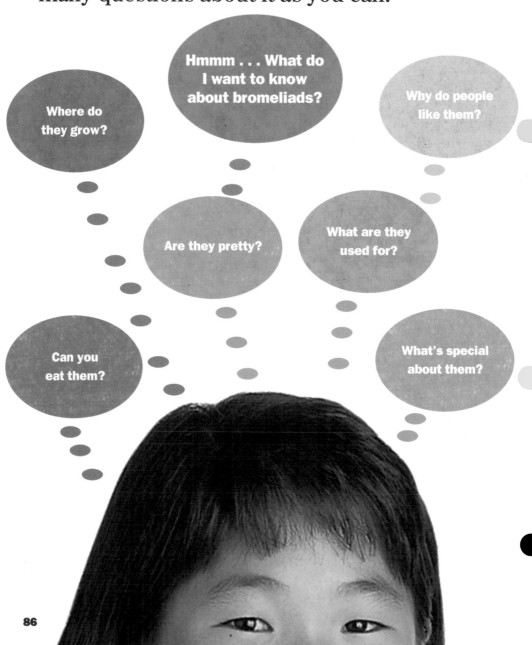

Find the Facts

You can always count on finding information in books, magazines, and newspapers, but dig deeper for new and unusual sources.

Go Places

Visit a botanical society or natural history museum.

Check It Out

Check the video store or library for documentary movies or TV programs on tropical or rainforest plants.

Roll the Tape

Interview people who know a lot about your topic—a plant specialist from a local university or even your neighbor who loves orchids.

Surf the Net

Try different search engines, bookmark favorite sites, and click on links to related sites. Print out any information you plan to use.

Map It Out

Once you have some information, mapping it out can help you organize your report.

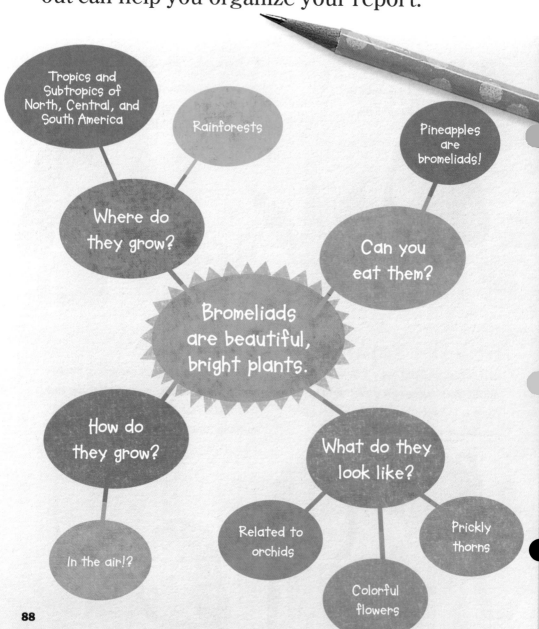

Tropics and Subtropics of North, Central, and South America

Rainforests

Pineapples are bromeliads!

Where do they grow?

Can you eat them?

Bromeliads are beautiful, bright plants.

How do they grow?

What do they look like?

In the air!?

Related to orchids

Colorful flowers

Prickly thorns

BIG
Truth

↓

Reports are just good stories.

Good stories teach people something
and entertain them, too.

Write It!

Grab 'Em

Introduce your topic and capture your reader's interest in the opening paragraph. Try an interesting fact or an intriguing quotation.

Make It Easy to Follow

Explore answers to your questions, and back up your main points. Remember to . . .

- **Organize. Present ideas in an order that makes sense, such as from big to little or in the order that things happen.**
- **Give details. Use specific examples to explain your point.**

Bromeliads by Amanda Jungles

Ouch! Be careful when you get near a bromeliad. Many of these tropical plants have sharp thorns on their leaves.

Bromeliads are air plants, or aroids. Their roots attach to tree trunks or branches, and they get their food from the air or rain. They have scales on their leaves that they use to catch and absorb water and other nutrients. They take in food from a little "cup" found in the middle of their leaves.

Bromeliads are members of the pineapple family, called Bromeliaceae. About two thousand species and 46 different kinds of bromeliads have been found. They can measure from cm (about 1 in.) to about live in dense rainforests like the Amazon. Some need a lot of rain, and others are able to use fog as their main source of moisture.

All bromeliads have flowers. They come in a lot of colors. Some are so beautiful that people keep them as houseplants. Other bromeliads have tiny flowers that you can't see, and some flowers are hidden by leaves. Bromeliads are very close in species to orchids.

Did you know that bromeliads are great breeding places for mosquitos? The mosquitos actually put their larvae in the little water pouches where the flowers are.

So the next time you are in the rainforest or your backyard, keep an eye out for beautiful bromeliads— but watch out for prickly leaves and mosquitos.

■ Keep it short. Don't try to impress with long words and sentences. The shorter the sentence or word, the easier it can be to get your point across.

■ Be yourself. Use words that you would use when talking to a friend.

■ Explain. Instead of just saying something happens, describe how it happens.

The End

Make sure you leave the reader with a clear understanding of your topic and tie up all your loose ends.

Who's Talking?

Copying text word for word from another source and not giving reference for it is like stealing someone's voice. And most teachers can tell when *Encyclopedia Britannica* is talking and not you.

Make It Great!

Get creative with your presentation.

Design a **stamp.**

Compose and sing a song.

Make a scrapbook or photo album.

Design a **T-shirt.**

Write and design a newspaper, travel brochure, or Web site.

Videotape a mock TV interview.

Draw a comic book.

Design a flag.

Create trading or recipe cards.

Create a walking billboard.

Design a roadside billboard.

Write an "A-to-Z" guide.

Throw a party.

Wow the Crowd

Present your report with style.

Shake the Jitters

Get rid of any jitters before your report by making a list of "what ifs" and coming up with solutions. If something does go wrong, you'll be prepared.

Rehearse

Practice, practice! Give your report in front of a mirror, to your dad, even into a tape recorder. The more familiar you are with what you want to say, the more smoothly it will go—and the more confident you'll feel.

Props

Bring props, such as maps, photos, or music, to share with your classmates.

Fluster Buster

Don't get flustered if you make a mistake while you're speaking. Just think "It's not a big deal," correct yourself, and move on.

Body Language

Make eye contact with your audience and smile. Try not to stand frozen in one place. Move around and use your hands when you speak.

Dress Up

Wear your favorite outfit so you'll look good for your audience and feel good about yourself. Or dress in a costume related to your report.

Zap the Zzzz's!

Keep your audience awake simply by being excited about your topic. A little humor never hurts, either!

hee!

hee!

ha!

ha!

hal

hee!

**School's out! School's out!
Watch all the kids run out.
Some go east. Some go west.
You'll go on to do your best!**